The Ultimate Chicken Wing Cookbook

Cajun Chicken Wings

12		Chicken wings -- tips removed
5		Bay leaves -- crumbled into bits
3/4	teaspoon	Caraway seeds
1/2		To 3/4 tsp. cayenne pepper
3/4	teaspoon	Ground cumin
3/4	teaspoon	Ground coriander
4		Garlic cloves -- finely
1 1/2	teaspoons	Dry mustard
2	teaspoons	Paprika -- preferably
3/4	teaspoon	Dried thyme leaves
1/2	teaspoon	Salt
2	tablespoons	Brandy
2	tablespoons	Fresh lemon or lime juice

Defat the chicken wings by cooking them in boiling water for 10 minutes. Drain and set aside to cool. Preheat oven to 375 degrees. Using a large mortar and pestle, grind together the bay leaf bits, caraway seeds, cayenne pepper, coriander, cumin, garlic, mustard, paprika, thyme and salt for about 10 minutes. Add the brandy and lemon or lime juice to the pulverized herbs and stir into a thick paste. With a pastry brush, cover both sides of each wing with the herb paste. When no more remains in the mortar, squeeze the last few drops from the brush. Arrange the chicken wings on a baking sheet. Bake until the skin turns deep brown and is quite crisp approximately 30 minutes. Takes about an hour to prepare.

AFRICAN CHICKEN WINGS

FOR THE WINGS
- 4 Garlic cloves
- 2 Shallots
- 1 1/2 teaspoons Salt
- 1 tablespoon Chinese 5 spice
- 2 teaspoons Paprika
- 1 teaspoon Dried rosemary -- crumbled
- 1/2 teaspoon Cayenne -- or to taste
- 2 tablespoons Vegetable oil
- 4 pounds Chicken wings -- about 20-24 Tips removed

FOR THE SAUCE
- 1/3 cup Natural style peanut butter
- 1/4 cup Canned cream of coconut -- Well stirred
- 2 Garlic cloves -- chopped
- 1/4 cup Water
- 1/4 cup Red bell pepper -- chopped
- 1/8 teaspoon Dried hot red pepper flakes Or to taste
- 1 teaspoon Soy sauce
- Coriander sprigs

THE WINGS: Prepare the chicken wings: Mince and mash the garlic and shallots to a paste with the salt. In a large bowl stir the paste together with the 5 spice powder, paprika, rosemary, cayenne, and the oil. Mix well. Add the chicken wings. Toss and stir them until they are completely covered with the marinade. Let them marinate, covered and chilled for 4 hours or over night. Arrange the wings, skin side up, on the rack of a foil lined large broiler pan and bake them in the upper third of a preheated 425F oven for 25 to 30 minutes or until they are golden. The wings may be prepared one day in advance, kept covered and chilled and then reheated before serving. THE SAUCE: In a blender, blend together the peanut butter, cream of coconut, garlic, water, bell pepper, red pepper flakes and the soy sauce until the mixture is smooth, season the sauce with salt, to taste. THE PRESENTATION:
Transfer the sauce to a serving bowl set on a platter.
Arrange the wings around the bowl and garnish the platter with the coriander.

Anchor Bar Hot Wings

Chicken wings Read below

The key to good Buffalo Wings is how you prepare them as well as the ingredients and the handling of the wings. The most successful wings served up here in Buffalo are what they call "Grade A Grinders." Fresh wings that are very large and meaty. Usually, you cannot get them in a frozen package, but can get them from a poultry dealer. Once you find them make sure they are absolutely fresh. Wash them in cold water, split them at the joint and remove the tips. Place them on a rack on a pan and refrigerate overnight to let the blood and water drain out of the wings.
THIS IS A REAL KEY. Drying the wings under refrigeration will help to make them a much crispier product, once deep fried. Next, use a deep fryer or a very heavy deep pot with a thermometer and add the oil. Peanut oil is very good, or a commercial product such as can be found at a restaurant cash and carry called Mel Fry. Heat the oil up SLOWLY, to 365F, and depending on the size of the fryer, deep fry the dry wings 6-8 minutes in small batches, until thoroughly done and golden brown. Hold the cooked wings in a warm oven if necessary. A combination of melted margarine and hot sauce in the ratio of 1 part margarine to 3 parts hot sauce will add the right zing. The key here is to add just enough sauce to coat the wings - the more sauce you add, the hotter they will be. For the very brave, 1 part margarine to 3 parts hot sauce and 1 part Tabasco is referred to as "Suicidal Wings" by the late and dear Don Bellissimo, who owned the Anchor Bar.
Working quickly, place the deep fried wings in a large bowl and add the sauce mixture, shaking to coat them.
There are many good hot sauces to use; the one they use is either Durkee Franks Red Hot Sauce or Wingers Original, again found in a restaurant cash and carry.
Celery sticks and chunky blue cheese dressing (Ken's Buffalo Style Blue Cheese is a popular one) and plenty of napkins.

Barbecue Wing Dings

3	pounds	chicken wing
3	tablespoons	brown sugar
2	drops	Worcestershire sauce
4	cups	ketchup
1		onion

Cut off the small piece of the chicken wing and the bony part so you have only the meaty part. Mix the ketchup, onion (cut up), brown sugar and sauce together. Dip wings in the sauce. Put on cookie sheet. Bake at 350 degrees for about 1 1/2 hour. If you have extra sauce, cook in saucepan until thick.

Barbecued Chicken Wings

35		Chicken wings -- tips removed
1		Stick butter
1	cup	Brown sugar
1/2	tablespoon	Sauce
1/2	cup	Dry red wine
2	teaspoons	Dry mustard
2	large	Garlic cloves -- crushed
1/4	cup	Fresh lemon juice
		Fresh ground pepper to taste

Requires marinating and long cooking time but it is simple. Place chicken wings, disjointed, in large flat pan. Combine other ingredients and pour over chicken.

Let stand for at least 1 hour or overnight. Be sure all wings are well coated with marinade. Place pan in 350 oven and reduce heat to 250. Bake 4-5 hours, turning wings at regular intervals. If all marinade is not absorbed, pour off and dry wings out a bit longer in oven (but not too much) before serving.

Beau's Sweet-Sour Chicken Wings

20		Chicken wings
7 1/2	ounces	Tomato sauce (half can)
2	tablespoons	Orange marmalade
1	tablespoon	Honey
2	teaspoons	Ginger -- minced
2	teaspoons	Fermented chili sauce -- (Summit brand)
2	teaspoons	Pepper vinegar
4		Garlic cloves -- peeled
1	teaspoon	Salt (scant)
2	teaspoons	MSG
1/2	cup	Water (more as needed)

ds Tabasco, to taste -(or other hot pepper
-sauce)

Cut off spurs from chicken wing-tips and rinse chicken wings. Place in pressure cooker with water; bring to pressure and cook at high heat for up to five minutes. Remove from pressure cooker and place cooked-out fat in wide-mouthed, tapered jar for other uses.

Blend all ingredients except chicken and Tabasco (or hot sauce) until fairly even consistency, with no large chunks of ginger or garlic.

Place 3/4 of sauce in pan. Roll wings in sauce; remove wings to broiler pan (with slotted top). Bake at 325 degrees F. for 20 minutes. Remove from oven and spoon about half of remaining sauce on top of each piece; broil for 5 minutes. Add Tabasco or other hot pepper sauces to taste and serve.

Beau's notes:

* Use vinegar "which has been used to keep a supply of bird's-eye peppers."
* After discarding chicken spurs, wash hands with very warm water and Dial soap (and follow up with isopropyl alcohol rinse); wash all utensils with bleach. (One should always regard chickens, even if processed in USA or inspected by USDA, as unclean! USDA inspectors are notoriously less than thorough, and U.S. packing houses often neglect basic hygienic rules in working with chickens, especially in dealing with their entrails, waste products un-excreted, etc. And one should not expect much better from out-of-country chickens.)

-

BEAUJOLAIS-GLAZED CHICKEN WINGS

- 3 pounds   Chicken wings -- tips removed at joints into 2 pcs
- 1/3 cup   Soy sauce
- 1/3 cup   Orange juice
- 2/3 cup   Dry red wine
- 2 tablespoons   Dry red wine -- (additional)
- 3   Cloves garlic -- mashed
- 2 tablespoons   Ginger root -- chopped
- 6 tablespoons   Red currant jelly
- 2 tablespoons   Orange zest -- grated
- 1 tablespoon   Orange zest -- thin julienne For garnish

1. Place split wings in a large shallow nonaluminum pan. Mix soy, orange juice, red wine, garlic and ginerrroot together and pour over the wings. Cover pan with plastic wrap and refrigerate overnight, turning several times in the marinade. 2. 375. Line a baking pan with foil. Coat a cooking cooking spray and place rack in baking pan. 3. Drain chicken and arrange on once. Remove from oven, but do not turn off the oven.
4. Combine jelly, 2 T Stir until jelly is melted.
Brush wings generously with the glaze and return to oven for 10 minutes. Turn and brush again with glaze.
Bake another 10 minutes, or until a rich dark brown and shiny. Remove and cool minutes. Can be baked up to a day ahead and reheated. 5. Arrange in overlap

Betty White's Chicken Wings Pacifica

- 3 pounds chicken wings
- 1/2 cup butter or margarine
- 1 cup soy sauce
- 1 cup brown sugar
- 3/4 cup water
- 1/2 teaspoon dry mustard

Arrange wings in shallow baking pan. Heat butter, soy sauce, sugar, water and mustard until butter and sugar melt. Cool; pour over wings and marinate at least 2 hours, turning once or twice. Bake in same pan at 375: for 1-1/4 to 1-1/2 hours, turning occasionally. Drain on paper towels.

Blue Cheese Dip

- 2 ounces — Blue cheese -- crumbled
- 1/2 cup — Sour cream
- 1/2 cup — Mayonnaise

Place everything in food processor and process till smooth. Chill.   Serve with celery sticks and Buffalo Chicken Wings

BLUE CORNMEAL CHICK WINGS

1/4	cup	Lime juice
1/4	cup	Oil
1/2	teaspoon	Crushed red pepper
10		Chicken wings -- about 2 lb
2	tablespoons	Margarine or butter
1/2	cup	Blue or yellow cornmeal
2	tablespoons	Flour
1/2	teaspoon	Salt
1/2	teaspoon	Ground cumin
1/8	teaspoon	Pepper

Mix lime juice, oil and red pepper in large glass or plastic bowl. Cut eac chicken wing at joints to make 3 pieces. Discard tip. Cut off and discard excess skin.

Place wings in oil mixture and stir to coat. Cover and refrig 3 hours, stirring occasionally. Drain. Heat oven to 425F. Heat margarine Shake remaining ingredients in plastic bag or mix in bowl. Shake wings in cornmeal mixture to coat and place in pan. Bake, uncovered, 20 minutes. Turn. Bake until golden brown, 20 to 25 minutes longer.

Broiled Chicken Wings

1	pound	chicken wings
3	tablespoons	lemon juice
3	tablespoons	soy sauce
1/8	teaspoon	onion powder
		salt -- to taste
		pepper -- to taste
1	tablespoon	honey
1	tablespoon	catsup

Remove tips from wings; cut wings into 2 pieces, and place in a shallow dish. Combine lemon juice, soy sauce, and onion powder; pour over chicken. Cover and marinate wings in refrigerator several hours or overnight. Drain chicken wings, reserving 1 tablespoon marinade; place wings on a foil-lined broiler pan. Sprinkle with salt and pepper. Combine reserved marinade, honey, and catsup, stirring well; brush half of mixture on chicken wings. Broil 6 to 7 inches from broiler for 7 minutes. Turn and brush with remaining sauce; broil 7 additional minutes.

BRONZED CHICKEN WINGS WITH YOUNG GINGER

2	pounds	Chicken wings
1/4	cup	Dark corn syrup
1/4	cup	Soy sauce
1	tablespoon	Corn oil
2	teaspoons	Minced fresh ginger
2	tablespoons	Dry sherry
1/4	pound	Very small mushrooms
1/2		Sliced bamboo shoots
2		Green onions -- cut in 2"
1/2	cup	Chicken broth
1	tablespoon	Cornstarch
2	tablespoons	Water

Cut wing tips off chicken wings. Place in shallow baking dish. In small bowl, stir together corn syrup and soy sauce. Pour over chicken wings; toss to coat well. Marinate 30 minutes. Drain; reserve marinade.

In large heavy skillet, heat corn oil over medium heat. Add chicken wings and ginger; stir fry 2 minutes. Stir in reserved marinade and sherry. Add mushrooms, bamboo shoots and green onions; stirring frequently, cook 2 minutes. Add chicken broth. Bring to boil. Reduce heat; cover and simmer 20 minutes or until tender. Remove chicken wings to serving platter, keep warm.

Stir together cornstarch and water until smooth. Stir into skillet. Stirring constantly, bring to boil over medium heat and boil 1 minute. Spoon over chicken wings. Makes 4 servings.

Buffalo Chicken Wings

3	pounds	Chicken wings -- Salt and pepper
1		Bottle Crystal's sauce
	-----FOR DIP-----	
1	ounce	Crumbled bleu cheese
1/3	cup	Mayonnaise
2	tablespoons	Milk
		Celery sticks

Lop the tips off the chicken wings and cut into drummettes. Discard tips or use for stock. Bake drummettes in a flat pan at 350 degrees for 25 minutes. Drain pan juices into stock pot for future use. Add Crystal's Sauce, either medium or hot, and cook another 20 minutes. Prepare dip by mixing and arrange all on a platter while piping hot. The wings are traditionally served with bleu cheese and celery.

BUFFALO CHICKEN WINGS #2

2	pounds	Chicken Wings
		Oil For Frying
1/2	cup	Butter
1	tablespoon	Tabasco Sauce
1	tablespoon	Hot Pepper Sauce
		Blue Cheese Dressing
		Chilled Celery Sticks

Fry up the chicken wings that have had the tips removed and cut in half at the joint in 1/4 cup of butter until golden brown. Allow the wings to cool before frying a second time, yes they are fried a second time so if you are a calorie watcher you can stop now. They can be fried the first time a day ahead. Before frying the second time mix the Tabasco and Hot Pepper sauce with the melted butter. Fry the wings a second time in the HOT butter until wings are heated. You need to use enough Tabasco and Hot Pepper sauce to give the butter a reddish color. Serve with chilled celery sticks and blue cheese dressing.

BUFFALO CHICKEN WINGS #3

2	pounds	Chicken Wings
		Salad Oil
1	tablespoon	Tabasco Sauce
1/4	cup	Melted Butter
		Celery Sticks
		Carrot Sticks
		Blue Cheese Dressing

Cut tips off wings and cut wing in half at the joint. In a 4 quart saucepan, heat 2 inches of salad oil to 375oF. Lower wings into oil. Fry chicken wings for 15 minutes or until very tender. Drain on paper towel. Meanwhile, in a large bowl, stir together Tabasco Sauce and butter until well blended. Add the chicken wings and toss gently to coat well. Serve with blue cheese dressing, chilled celery sticks and chilled carrot sticks.

BUFFALO CHICKEN WINGS #4

1/2	cup	Miracle Whip
1/4	cup	Sour Cream
1/4	pound	Blue Cheese
4		Ribs Celery
1		Small Onion
2		Cloves Garlic
1	tablespoon	Oil
1/2		Lemon
8	ounces	Tomato Sauce
1/4	cup	Tabasco Sauce
1/2	teaspoon	Salt
3	pounds	Chicken Wings
		Oil For Frying

Combine Miracle Whip and sour cream. Crumble and stir in the blue cheese. Cut the celery into sticks. Chop onion and mince garlic. Cook onion in oil over medium heat until soft, about 2 minutes. Add the garlic and cook for one more minute. Squeeze in the juice from the lemon. Stir in tomato sauce, Tabasco and salt.
Cook for 5 minutes. Remove wing tips and cut wings in half at the joint. Heat oil for deep frying to 375oF.
Cook wings in hot oil until brown, about 8 minutes.
Toss wings in tomato mixture. Serve with chilled celery sticks and blue cheese dressing.

BUFFALO CHICKEN WINGS #5

1/2	cup	Miracle Whip
1/4	cup	Sour Cream
1/4	pound	Blue Cheese
4		Ribs Celery
1		Small Onion
2		Cloves Garlic
1	tablespoon	Oil
1/2		Lemon
8	ounces	Tomato Sauce
1/4	cup	Tabasco Sauce
1/2	teaspoon	Salt
3	pounds	Chicken Wings
		Oil For Frying

Combine Miracle Whip and sour cream. Crumble and stir in the blue cheese. Cut the celery into sticks. Chop onion and mince garlic. Cook onion in oil over medium heat until soft, about 2 minutes. Add the garlic and cook for one more minute. Squeeze in the juice from the lemon. Stir in tomato sauce, Tabasco and salt.
Cook for 5 minutes. Remove wing tips and cut wings in half at the joint. Heat oil for deep frying to 375oF.
Cook wings in hot oil until brown, about 8 minutes.
Toss wings in tomato mixture. Serve with chilled celery sticks and blue cheese dressing.

BUFFALO CHICKEN WINGS #6

2	pounds	Chicken Wings
		Tabasco Sauce
1/4	pound	Butter
		Blue Cheese Dressing
		Chilled Celery Sticks
		Chilled Carrot Sticks

Remove tips from wings. Cut wings in half at the joint. Deep-fry in hot oil until golden, about 5 minutes or bake the wings in a 375oF oven for 30-40 minutes until browned. Melt butter and combine with Tabasco Sauce. Add whatever quantity of Tabasco Sauce suits your HOT Button. Coat the wings with the HOT Butter mixture and serve with blue cheese dressing and chilled celery and carrot sticks.

BUFFALO CHICKEN WINGS W/ BLUE CHEESE DIPPING SAUCE

6	tablespoons	Butter or margarine
1/4	cup	Hot pepper sauce
		Vegetable oil for frying
18		Chicken wings, disjointed -- tips discarded
		Dipping Sauce:
1/4	pound	Blue cheese -- Roquefort or
1/2	cup	Mayonnaise
1/2	cup	Sour cream
1	tablespoon	Lemon juice
1	tablespoon	Wine vinegar

hot pepper sauce to taste

Prep: 10 minutes Cook: 35 minutes Serves: 36 mini-drumsticks

These spicy hot wings w/ cool, creamy dip are all the rage. Serve w/ plenty of ice-cold beer.

1. Melt butter in a small saucepan. Add hot sauce & remove from the heat.

2. In large frying pan or deep-fat fryer, heat 1" of oil to 375ø. Fry wings in batches w/o crowding until golden brown, 12 1/2 minutes. Drain on paper towels.

3. Brush wings w/ spicy butter & serve warm w/ Blue Cheese dipping sauce.

BLUE CHEESE DIPPING SAUCE
In small bowl, mash the blue cheese, leaving some small lumps. Whisk in the mayonnaise until blended. Add the remaining ingredients & whisk to blend well. Cover & refrigerate until serving time.

BUFFALO CHICKEN WINGS WITH BLUE CHEESE DIPPING SAUCE 2

```
                -----CHICKEN WINGS-----
  6     tablespoons  Butter
   1/4  cup          Hot pepper sauce
                Vegetable oil -- for frying
 18              Chicken wings (about 3lb) -- disjointed with tips
                -----BLUE CHEESE DIPPING SAUCE-----
   1/4  pound        Blue cheese -- roquefort or

   1/2  cup          Mayonnaise
   1/2  cup          Sour cream
  1     tablespoon   Lemon juice
  1     tablespoon   Wine vinegar
```

ds Hot pepper sauce

1. Melt butter in a small saucepan. Add hot sauce and remove from heat.

2. In large frying pan or deep-fat fryer, heat 1 inch of oil to 375F. Fry wings in batches without crowding until golden brown, 10 to 15 minutes.
Drain on paper towels.

3. Brush wings with spicy butter and serve warm, with blue cheese dipping sauce.

Sauce:

In a small bowl, mash the blue cheese, leaving some clumps. Whisk in the mayonnaise until blended. Add remaining ingredients and whisk to blend well. Cover and refrigerate until serving time.

Buffalo Wings, from Buffalo N.Y.

4	pounds	Chicken wings
3	tablespoons	Butter -- melted
3	tablespoons	Worcestershire sauce
2	teaspoons	Catsup
2		Garlic cloves -- mashed

-----DIP-----

2/3	cup	Mayonnaise
1/3	cup	Sour cream
1/3	cup	Gorgonzola
		OR bleu cheese
1/2	teaspoon	Tabasco
		Celery stalks

Cut off tip of wing. Separate at joint. Place on wire rack in roasting pan. Roast at 350 deg. for 1 1/2 hours. Turn once during cooking. Combine melted butter, Tabasco, Worcestershire, catsup, garlic and mix well in large bowl. Place chicken in bowl and mix well. Crumble cheese coarsely and mix with other dip ingredients in separate bowl and serve with celery stalks and wings.

CAJUN CHICKEN WINGS

- 2 1/2 pounds   Chicken wings -- separated an
- 3/4 cup   Plain yogurt
- 2/3 cup   Louisiana hot sauce.
- 2 teaspoons   Garlic powder
- 1 cup   Flour
- 1/2 cup   Cajun seasoning
- Oil -- for frying

In a bowl, mix together yogurt, hot sauce and garlic. Add chicken and marinate overnight in the refrigerator. The following day, mix together flour and cajun seasonings in a bowl. Remove chicken from the marinade and coat evenly in flour mixture. In a wok or deep fryer, heat oil to 370F.
This can be achieved by heating over medium high heat. Use enough oil to cover 4 to 5 chicken wings at a time. Deep fry wings for approximately 8 minutes. Drain on paper towel. Serves 2 to 4

CAMPBELL'S HONEY MUSTARD WINGS

1	pound	Campbell's dry onion with ch Soup and recipe mix -- dry
1/2	cup	Honey
1/4	cup	Spicy brown mustard
16		Chicken wings -- whole or cut
		Season-all -- to taste

1. In a large bowl, combine soup mix, honey, and mustard. Set aside.

2. Cut wings at joints and discard the tips, or leave the wings whole. Add chicken to soup mixture. Toss to coat.

3. Place chicken in a baking pan greased with Pam spray. Sprinkle with Season-All. Bake at 375 degrees F for about 1 hour or until chicken is don turning once if desired. If wings are getting too brown too soon, cover with tin foil during the latter part of baking time.

Can't Get Enough Chicken Wings

    12   chicken wings (2 lbs.)
     1/2 cup   margarine or butter -- melted
    1   envelope   Lipton recipe
                   secrets savory herb with
                   garlic recipe soup mix
    1   teaspoon   cayenne pepper sauce -- opt'l
                   to taste

Cut tips off chicken wings (save tips for soup.) Cut chicken wings in half at joint. Deep fry, bake or broil until golden brown and crunchy. In medium bowl, blend margarine, savory herb with garlic recipe soup mix and cayenne pepper sauce. Add more or less cayenne pepper to match your 'hot & spicy tolerance level. Add chicken wings; toss until coated. Serve over greens with cut-up celery, if desired. Makes 24 appetizers.

Center Club Chicken Wings

4	pounds	chicken wings
1 1/4	cups	hoisin sauce
3/4	cup	plum sauce
1/2	cup	soy sauce
1/3	cup	cider vinegar
1/4	cup	dry sherry
1/4	cup	honey
6		green onions -- minced
6	cloves	garlic -- minced

Cut off and discard wing tips. Separate wing at joint. At the drumstick joint, separate bones with small knife and push meat to tip. Remove smaller bone and discard. Mix all other ingred in large bowl. Add chicken and coat well. After refrigerating coated chicken for at least 24 hrs, preheat oven to 375 degrees. Line baking pan with foil and place rack over foil, first coating rack with cooking spray. Drain chicken, reserving liquid. Place chicken on rack and roast for 30 min. Baste, turn wings and return to oven for an additional 30 min.

CHICKEN WING DRUMSTICKS

10		Chicken wings (yield 20 "Drumsticks)
1		Egg white -- slightly beaten
1/3	cup	Cornstarch--mixed with:
1	teaspoon	Baking powder
		Peanut oil for deep frying

-----MARINADE-----

1	teaspoon	Five-spice powder
1/2	teaspoon	MSG (optional)
1	teaspoon	Salt
1/2	teaspoon	Sugar
1	teaspoon	Rice wine
1	teaspoon	Soy sauce

Discard wing tips. Cut between joints. Remove the smaller bone of the lower wing. Cut skin loose around the small end and push skin and meat up to form drumstick.

Marinate wings for 1 hour. Add egg white. Coat wings evenly. (Using egg white to coat the wings will help to seal the juice inside the meat. Hence the meat will be juicier.

Dredge wings in cornstarch mixture. (Using cornstarch and baking powder helps to make the outside layer crisp.) Deep-fry for 3 minutes. Drain. Let cool.

Deep-fry once again right before serving. (Deep-fry the first time to cook the meat and seal the juice in the meat. The second time to make the outside crisp.
Make sure the oil is very hot before you deep-fry for the second time.)

Chicken Wings

1	package	Chicken Wings
1	cup	Coca-Cola
1	cup	Catsup
1/4	cup	Butter

Put wings in baking dish. Mix ingredients and pour over them. Bake in a 325oF oven until done, approximately 1 hour.

Chicken Wings In Five Spice

12		chicken wings -- whole
1	cup	water-chestnut flour
4	cups	peanut oil for deep-frying
		marinade:
1/2	teaspoon	freshly grated ginger
1/8	cup	light soy sauce
1/8	cup	dry sherry or chinese rice -- wine
1/2	teaspoon	five-spice powder

Cut each wing into 3 logical pieces. Save the tips for soup and use only the 2 meatier parts for this recipe. Prepare the marinade and marinate the wing pieces for 1/2 hour. Drain and toss in the water-chestnut flour. Deep-fry at 360 F until golden brown, about 5 minutes.

CHICKEN WINGS IN OYSTER SAUCE

- 1 Chicken wings
- 3 slices Fresh ginger root
- Vegetable oil
- 4 tablespoons Oyster sauce
- 1 tablespoon Dry sherry
- 1/2 teaspoon Sugar
- 2 1/2 tablespoons Soy sauce
- 1 cup Water

Cut each wing into two pieces by separating at the joint; discard the tips. Heat the ginger slices in the oil in a wok; add a third of the wings at a time and brown. When the wings are browned, drain the oil and remove the ginger slices from the wok. Add the oyster sauce, sherry, sugar soy sauce, and water. Place the browned wings in the wok and simmer, covered, for 10 to 1 minutes. Cook another 12 to 15 minutes with the lid off, basting frequently with the sauce. When the wings are tender and nicely glazed, they are ready to be eaten.

CHICKEN WINGS PACIFICA

45		Chicken wings
2	cups	Soy sauce
2	cups	Brown sugar -- packed
1	cup	Butter
2	teaspoons	Dry mustard
1 1/2	cups	Water

Disjoint chicken wings, discarding bony tips. Arrange meatier wing parts in shallow baking pan. Combine soy sauce, brown sugar, butter, mustard and water and heat until sugar and butter dissolve. Cool and pour over wings.

Marinate in refrigerator 2 hours, turning occasionally. Bake, in marinade, at 350 degrees 45 minutes, turning once and spooning marinade over chicken occasionally. Drain on paper towels and serve hot or cold.
Note: Marinade goes along way. More wings can be added. Marinate in 2 large ziplock bags.

Chicken Wings W/sauce

8		Chicken -- wings-washed
1/4	cup	Veg oil
1	teaspoon	Garlic; -- chopped
3	teaspoons	Soy sauce -- sweet dark
1/4	teaspoon	Msg -- optional
1	cup	Water
1		Onion -- sliced
1	teaspoon	Ginger -- finely chopped fres
2		Green onion -- cut 1" pcs.

Directions: Cook chicken wings in water on high heat for 10-12 minutes. Add oil and cook for 15 minutes on medium heat or until chicken is brown on both sides. Reduce heat to med high, drizzle all wings with sweet dark soy sauce one tbsp at a time. Stir 4 or 5 times. Make sure that all wings are coated. Add remaining ingredients. Simmer on low heat for 5-8 minutes. Remove from heat. Let stand3-4 minutes. Serve warm with hot cooked rice.

Chilled Chilied Chicken Wings

2	tablespoons	HOT CHILI POWDER
2		WHOLE EGGS LIGHTLY BEATEN
4	pounds	CHICKEN WINGS (15)
		OIL FOR FRYING
1/2	cup	BOILING WATER
1	tablespoon	CUMIN
2	tablespoons	KETCHUP
2	tablespoons	HOT PAPRIKA
1 1/2	tablespoons	HOT PEPPER SAUCE
1	teaspoon	OREGANO
1	teaspoon	SALT
1/2	teaspoon	FRESH GROUND PEPPER

MIX THE CHILI POWDER,CUMIN,HOT PAPRIKA,OREGANO,SALT
AND PEPPER TOGETHER WITH THE BOILING WATER,AND STIR
TO MAKE A CHILI PASTE. STIR IN TH KETCHUP AND PEPPER
SAUCE.SET ASIDE TO COOL SLIGHTLY.PLACE THE EGGS IN
A LARGE BOWL,AND STIR IN THE CHILI PASTE.MIX WELL.
CUT THE TAPERED JOINT FROM THE WINGS,AND RESERVE
FOR STOCK OR ANOTHER USE.PUT THE TRIMMED WINGS IN
THE SPICE EGG MIXTURE.TOSS THROUGHLY.THE WINGS SHOULD
SOAK IN THE MARINADE FOR SEVERAL HOURS IN THE
REFRIGERATOR;THE LONGER THEY MARINATE,THE SPICER
THEY WILL BE.HEAT AN INCH OF OIL IN A HEAVY SKILLET
TO 375 DEGREES.(IT'S THE PROPER TEMPERATURE WHEN A
WING TIP DIPPED IN THE OIL CAUSES AN IMMEDIATE
BUBBLING) FRY THE WINGS IN BATCHES FOR ABOUT EIGHT
MINUTES,FLIPPING ONCE DURING COOKING.BE SURE NOT TO
CROWD THE PAN. DRAIN ON PAPER TOWELS.SERVE HOT OR CHILLED

CHINA SAM'S CHICKEN WINGS

1/4	cup	Lite Teriyaki Marinade
1/4	cup	Oriental BBQ Sauce -- Kikoman
1/4	cup	Lee Kum Kee -- (oyster sauce)
1	tablespoon	Brown sugar
12	medium	Chicken wings -- whole
1	teaspoon	Oriental Season -- Amyway
1	teaspoon	Hot & Spicy Stir Fry Season
1	teaspoon	Soy -- Kikoman

Separate drumette from rest of wing. Place on broiler pan skin side down. Season with Oriental Seasoning and Hot & Spicy Stir Fry Seasoning (from Calaphon). Place on middle rack of preheated oven to broil. As wings start to cook, begin making dipping sauce. Place Teriyaki, Oriental BBQ, Soy and brown sugar together, whisk. When wings start to color good, 10 minutes or so, remove from oven and turn over, season slightly, return to oven. When wings are Golden brown on this side, remove. Dip and shake of excess sauce. After all have been dipped return to broiler pan and return to oven. Let broil until a bit crusted, not more than a few minutes. Great as an appetizer or side dish with fried rice. Try with a glass of plum wine.

Chinese Chicken Wings

24		Chicken wings, separated -- tips discarded
2	cups	Soy sauce
2	teaspoons	Prepared mustard (the Asian -- kind not Frenches)
2	teaspoons	Freshly grated ginger
1/2	cup	Sugar
2	teaspoons	Finely chopped garlic

1. Combine soy, mustard, ginger, sugar and garlic, stir well, then pour over chicken wings,

2. Cover and refrigerate over night

3. At serving time heat oven to 350 degrees and bake for 1 hour or grill on a charcoal

COCONUT CURRIED WINGS

2		Dozen chicken wings
1/2	teaspoon	Coconut extract
4	teaspoons	Curry powder
6	tablespoons	Melted butter
1	cup	Milk
2	cups	Instant mashed potatoes
3	tablespoons	Sweetened -- flaked coconut
2		Cloves garlic -- minced

Cut tips off wings. In a large bowl, combine milk, extract and wings. Stir to mix well. Marinate at least 2 hours (or overnight). In another bowl, combine potatoes, curry and cocoanut. Take wings out of marinade and roll in potato mixture. Place slightly apart on well greased cookie sheets. Combine butter & garlic. Drizzle over wings. Bake, uncovered, at 375 degrees until browned - 45 minutes.

Cookie's Wings From Hell

4	cups	Hot sauce
2	tablespoons	Cayenne
		Chicken wings

To cut down the heat, use 1 Tb Ground Red pepper plus 1 Tb cayenne. Heat sauce as needed, for 10 minutes at 350, then dip wings into hot sauce mix. You can double the sauce recipe if you like. Use as much as you need to coat wings. You can strain what is left and reheat it and keep it in a jar. It will keep indefinitely. Just shake the jar and pour as much sauce as needed into a pan and reheat to dip chicken wings. The chef who gave me the recipe makes it a gallon at a time. He uses the cayenne-red pepper mix, I use all cayenne.

CREOLE CHICKEN WINGS WITH PEACH MUSTARD SAUCE

3	pounds	Chicken Wings
4		Cloves Garlic -- Minced
2	teaspoons	Dry Mustard
2	teaspoons	Paprika
1	teaspoon	Dried Thyme
1	teaspoon	Granulated Sugar
1	teaspoon	Cayenne Pepper
1/2	teaspoon	Salt
1/2	teaspoon	Black Pepper
1/4	cup	Lemon Juice

-----PEACH MUSTARD SAUCE-----

1/2	cup	Peach Jam
1	tablespoon	Dijon Mustard
2	teaspoons	Pimiento -- diced
1	teaspoon	Cider Vinegar

Cut tips off wings; reserve for stock. In small bowl, stir together garlic, mustard, paprika, thyme, sugar, cayenne, salt and black pepper; blend in lemon juice to make paste. Using pastry brush, brush paste over wings.

Arrange wings, meaty side down, on lightly greased foil-lined baking sheets. Let stand for 30 minutes at room temperature. Bake in 475F oven for 15 minutes; turn wings over and bake for 15 to 20 minutes or until brown, crisp and no longer pink inside.

Peach Mustard Sauce: In saucepan, melt jam over low heat; stir in mustard, pimiento and vinegar. Serve separately for dipping.

(Makes 4 main-course or 8 appetizer servings)

CRISPY ORIENTAL CHICKEN WINGS (MICROWAVE)

- 1 1/2 pounds chicken wings -- disjointed
- 1 medium egg
- 1/2 cup soy sauce
- 2 tablespoons garlic powder
- 1/4 teaspoon ginger powder
- 1 medium onion -- finely diced
- 2 cups finely crushed corn flakes

Mix together egg, soy sauce, garlic powder and ginger powder. Set aside.

On wax paper, mix together crushed corn flakes and diced onion. Dip each wing in soy sauce mixture, then roll in corn flakes and onion.

In glass baking dish, cover and cook wings on high (9) for 20 minutes, or until cooked. Remove covering halfway through cooking. Use 13"x9" baking dish. Yield: 24 appetizers.

CRISPY BUFFALO WINGS

   5   pounds   Chicken wings -- deep fried
 1/2 gallon   Hot pepper sauce
   1   cup   Cornstarch

Deep fry wings till over done. put in pan and cover w/ favorite hot sauce. tightly w/ foil and bake in over @ 300 for 1 hour. Cool completely in refrigerator. Roll wings in corn starch, dip in hot sauce again and roll in corn starch and let wings sit on plate for a few minutes.

Crispy Honey Wings

3/4	cup	honey
1/4	cup	white worcestershire sauce
1/2	teaspoon	ginger
3	pounds	chicken wings

Mix honey, worcestershire sauce and ginger. Grill chicken wings 4-6" from medium coals, 20-25 minutes, brushing frequently with honey mixture and turning after 10 minutes, until done. NOTE: If you can't find white worcestershire sauce, the dark colored variety can be used instead.

Crispy Honey Wings

3/4	Cup	Honey
1/4	Cup	White worcestershire sauce
1/2	Teaspoon	Ginger
3	Pounds	Chicken wings

Mix honey, worcestershire sauce and ginger. Grill chicken wings 4-6" from medium coals, 20-25 minutes, brushing frequently with honey mixture and turning after 10 minutes, until done.

NOTE: If you can't find white worcestershire sauce, the dark colored variety can be used instead.

Crunchy Parmesan Chicken Wings

4	pounds	Chicken wings
1/2	cup	Flour
1/2	teaspoon	Paprika
1/4	teaspoon	Salt and pepper
4		Eggs
2	cups	Parmesan cheese -- freshly gra
1/2	cup	Dry bread crumbs
1	teaspoon	Each dried basil and oregano

Remove tips from chicken wings and reserve for stock if desired; separate wings at joints. In shallow dish, combine flour, paprika, salt and pepper. In another shallow dish, beat eggs. In third shallow dish, combine cheese, bread crumbs, basil and oregano.

Dip wings into flour mixture, then into eggs, then into cheese mixture, pressing firmly. (Wings can be prepared to this point, placed on rack, covered and refrigerated for up to 4 hours.) Arrange wings on greased rimmed baking sheets. Bake in 375F oven for 35-40 minutes, turning once, or until golden brown and crisp. Makes about 60 pieces.

DRUMS OF HEAVEN

18		Chicken wings
3	ounces	Ginger root -- grated
1	ounce	Granulated garlic
1	teaspoon	Sesame oil
1	teaspoon	Salt
4	dashes	Tabasco
1	ounce	Brandy
1		Egg

-----SHRIMP BATTER-----

1	cup	Flour
2		Eggs
1/2	cup	Cornstarch
1	tablespoon	Baking powder
		Water

Wash chicken wings & cut away each tip section. Hold each end of a remaining, jointed wing, & disjoint by bending elbow; don't separate. Holding fingers tightly around smaller bone, press upward, pushing meat from smaller section right into larger section, giving wing a drumstick appearance. Repeat process with all wings.

Combine ginger root, garlic, oil, salt, Tabasco, brandy and egg in bowl & mix well. Marinate wings in mixture approximately 2-4 hrs. at room temperature.

Fold wings into Shrimp Batter; deep fry at 360 until golden brown.

BATTER: Combine all ingredients. Thin with water until the consistency is that of pancake batter For fluffier batter, add 1 tsp. oil & 4 oz. beer.

Easy Teriyaki Wings

- 1/4 cup Catsup
- 1/4 teaspoon Garlic powder
- 2 tablespoons Brown sugar
- 1/4 cup Oil
- 1/4 cup Soy sauce
- 1/4 cup Lemon juice
- 2 pounds Chicken wings

Remove wing tips from chicken and cut apart at joint.
Combine remaining ingredients. Marinate chicken in shallow baking dish overnight, turning occasionally.
Preheat oven to 375. Arrange chicken on rack in aluminum foil-lined shallow baking pan. Bake 40-45 minutes, basting occasionally with marinade.

Empress Chicken Wings

```
1 1/2  pounds      Chicken Wings
3      tablespoons Soy Sauce
1      tablespoon  Dry Sherry
1      tablespoon  Minced Fresh Ginger Root
1                  Clove Garlic -- Minced
2      tablespoons Vegetable Oil
  1/3  cup         Cornstarch
  2/3  cup         Water
2                  Green Onions And Tops -- Cut
                   Into Thin Slices
1      teaspoon    Slivered Fresh Ginger Root
```

Disjoint the chicken wings; discard tips (or save for stock). Combine soy sauce, sherry, minced ginger and garlic in a large bowl; stir in chicken. Cover and refrigerate for 1 hour, stirring occasionally. Remove chicken; reserve marinade. Heat oil in large skillet over medium heat. Lightly coat chicken pieces with cornstarch; add to skillet and brown slowly on all sides. Remove chicken; drain off fat. Stir water and reserved marinade into same skillet. Add chicken; sprinkle green onions and slivered ginger evenly over chicken. Cover and simmer for 5 minutes, or until chicken is tender.

Fajita Chicken Wings

12		Chicken wings
		marinade
1/4	cup	Lime juice
2	tablespoons	Oil
3	tablespoons	Cilantro -- chopped
1	Cl	Garlic -- minced
1	teaspoon	Cumin
1/2	teaspoon	Salt
1/2	teaspoon	Oregano
1/4	teaspoon	Red pepper flakes -- crushed

Cut each chicken wing in half; place in large resealable plastic bag. Add all marinade ingredients; seal bag. Turn bag to coat wings. Refrigerate at least 4 hours or up to 24 hours, turning bag occasionally.

Heat oven to 375 F. Drain chicken wings, reserving marinade. Place chicken on broiler pan. Bake at 375 F for 45 to 60 minutes or until chicken is no longer pink, brushing occasionally with reserved marinade.

Discard any remaining marinade.

Fajita Chicken Wings

12		Chicken wings -- tips removed

-----MARINADE-----

1/4	Cup	Lime juice
2	Tablespoons	Oil
3	Tablespoons	Fresh cilantro -- chopped
1		Garlic clove -- minced
1	Teaspoon	Cumin
1/2	Teaspoon	Salt
1/2	teaspoon	Dried oregano leaves
1/4	teaspoon	Crushed red pepper flakes

Cut each wing in half; place in large resealable bag. Add all marinade ingredients; seal bag. Turn bag to coat wings. Refrigerate at least 4 hours, up to 24 hours, turning bag occasionally. Heat oven to 375~. Drain chicken, reserving marinade. Place chicken on broiler pan. Bake 45-60 minutes, brushing occasionally with marinade. Discard any remaining marinade.

Finger Drumsticks

1 1/2 pounds	chicken wings - 12 to 15	
	salt and pepper	
1	cup	chicken bouillon
1	tablespoon	cornstarch
1/4	cup	sugar
1/2	teaspoon	salt
1/4	teaspoon	ground ginger
1/8	teaspoon	pepper
3	tablespoons	lemon juice
2	tablespoons	soy sauce
1/8	teaspoon	garlic salt

Cut off and discard wing tips; divide each wing in half by cutting through joint with a sharp knife. Sprinkle wings with salt and pepper. Place in slow-cooking pot. Pour bouillon over chicken. Cover and cook on low for 4 to 5 hours or until tender. Drain; place on broiler pan. Meanwhile, in small saucepan, combine cornstarch with sugar, salt, ginger, pepper, lemon juice, soy sauce and garlic salt. Simmer, stirring constantly, until mixture thickens. Brush some sauce on chicken; brown under broiler. Turn; brush sauce on chicken and brown other side. Makes about 25 to 30 appetizers. Recipe may be doubled for a party. Keep appetizers hot and serve from slow-cooking pot.

FIREY HOT CHICKEN WINGS

2 1/2	pounds	Chicken wings -- separated
5	tablespoons	Louisiana hot sauce
2	tablespoons	Vegetable oil
1	tablespoon	White vinegar
1/4	teaspoon	Garlic powder

These screaming hot chicken wings are easy to prepare, and can be made hot, hotter and scorching hot by adding more hot sauce. Enjoy these wings with celery sticks and Cool Cucumber Dip to help extinguish any "fires."
NOTE:
The recipe actually calls for 3 to 5 Tbsp of Louisiana hot sauce. Use your own discretion. Set oven to "broil" and place rack 6" from the element. In a medium sized mixing bowl combine hot sauce, oil, vinegar and garlic powder. Place chicken wings on a broiling pan. Using a pastry brush, coat the wings with the sauce mixture. Broil the wings for 7 minutes on one side before turning them over and broiling for another 7 minutes. You can also cook these wings over the BBQ. Cook wings for the same amount of time over medium high heat. Be sure to preheat the BBQ and brush the grill with oil to prevent sticking. Serves 2 - 4

Garlic Chicken Wings

* separated at joints; tips discarded in a strong plastic bag. Heat a large skillet with 2" of vegetable oil until hot. Shake wings in seasoned flour and fry until golden brown and crisp on both sides. Remove wings, drain on paper towels. When all wings are done, remove all but 2 Tblsp oil, leaving the browned bits on he bottom of the skillet. Add 3 Tblsp finely chopped garlic to the oil in the skillet and saute until soft, but not browned. Add 3/4 cup dry, Fino sherry into the skillet and scrape up the brown bits remaining. Add 1/2 cup chicken broth, stir and reduce the sauce by 1/3. It will become a bit thicker. Adjust seasoning with salt and pepper, return wings to sauce to heat briefly, coating with the sauce.

Garlicky Gilroy Chicken Wings

2	pounds	Chicken wings
15		Drops tabasco pepper sauce
3		Heads fresh garlic -- separated
1	cup	Grated parmesan cheese
		Into cloves and peeled
1	cup	Italian style bread crumbs
1	cup	Plus 1 T. olive oil -- divided
1	teaspoon	Black pepper

Preheat oven to 375. Disjoint chicken wings, removing tips. Rinse wings; pat dry. Place garlic, 1 cup oil and pepper sauce in food processor or blender container; cover and process until smooth. Pour garlic mixture into small bowl. Combine cheese, bread crumbs and black pepper in shallow dish.
Dip wings into garlic mixture, then roll, one at a time, in crumb mixture until thoroughly coated. Brush shallow nonstick pan with remaining 1 T. oil; arrange wings in a single layer. Drizzle remaining garlic mixture over wings; sprinkle with remaining crumb mixture. Bake 45 to 60 minutes or until brown and crisp. Garnish as desired.

Genuine Red Hot Buffalo Wings

3	cups	Durkee red hot cayenne pepper sauce
2	cups	Clarified butter -- hot
20	pounds	Chicken wings -- frozen

Deep-fry wings at 400F for 10 to 12 minutes until crispy brown or bake at 425? for 30 minutes; turn and bake additional 30 minutes, until brown. Drain well. Add to sauce and toss well to coat chicken wings. Keep warm. Serve with blue cheese dip and celery sticks. For added heat, try adjusting the ratio of Durkee Red hot Sauce to butter.

GERI'S HONEY CURRY CHICKEN WINGS

2	pounds	Chicken wings
1/2	cup	Butter
1/2	cup	Honey
1/4	cup	Prepared mustard
1	teaspoon	Salt
1	tablespoon	Curry (mild or hot)

place chicken in shallow baking pan, skin side up. Combine butter, honey, mustard, salt, & curry powder and mix well. Pour over chicken and bake at 350F for 1 1/4 hour's basting every 15 min's.

GLAZED CHICKEN WINGS

1	can	Cranberry jelly
1/4	cup	Water
3/4	cup	Grey Poupon -- honey style
1	teaspoon	Orange peel -- grated
16		Chicken wings, split -- with removed

Heat cranberry sauce and water over low heat, stirring occasionally until blended. Stir in mustard and orange peel. Remove from heat; cool slightly. In med. bowl, mix chicken with mustard mixture; cover and chill overnight.

Preheat oven to 400F. Remove chicken from marinade; reserve marinade. Arrange chicken on lightly greased foil-lined pan. Bake 40-45 minutes, turning and brushing chicken with marinade after 20 minutes.

Glazed Shoyu Chicken Wings

   1 1/2 pounds   Chicken wings
   3   Green onions -- cut in 2" piec
   3   tablespoons   Dry sherry
    1/4 cup   Dark soy sauce
   2   teaspoons   Sugar
                         Sesame seeds -- if desired

Remove tips from wings. Leave whole or cut at joint. Place onions in large wok or pan on medium heat. Stir in sherry and soy sauce. Add sugar and bring to a full boil. Reduce heat and place chicken in mixture. Cover and simmer over low heat for 20 minutes, turning occasionally or until done. Sprinkle sesame seeds if desired. Makes 8-10

Guerrini Chicken Wings

- 2 pounds chicken wings -- (to 3 lb)
- 1 1/2 teaspoons salt
- 7 tablespoons cornstarch
- 20 milliliters garlic -- minced
- 4 tablespoons flour
- 2 eggs
- 5 tablespoons soy sauce
- 4 tablespoons sugar
- 1 tablespoon toasted sesame seeds
- 2 green onions -- chopped
- oil for frying

Mix all ingredients except oil and chicken. Add chicken to mixture and marinate overnight in the refrigerator, turning occasionally to coat. Deep fry until golden brown.

Hawaiian Chicken Wings

2	pounds	chicken wings
1/4	cup	sugar
1/2	teaspoon	ginger -- ground
1/2	teaspoon	garlic powder
1/8	cup	onions -- chopped
1/4	teaspoon	black pepper
1/2	cup	soy sauce
6	ounces	pineapple juice

Remove wing tips from chicken and cut apart at joint. Combine remaining ingredients. Marinate chicken wings for at least 24 hours. Preheat oven to 375. Bake for 1 hour. Serve warm.

Hidden Valley Ranch Buffalo Wings

24		Chicken wings
1/2	cup	Melted butter
1/4	cup	Oriental hot pepper sauce
3	tablespoons	Vinegar
2	packages	Hidden valley ranch milk rec
		Original ranch salad dressin
1/2	teaspoon	Paprika
		Celery sticks

Preheat oven to 350 F degrees.

Dip chicken in mixture of melted butter, pepper sauce and vinegar, put in baking pan. Sprinkle with 1 package dry dressing mix. Bake 25 to 30 minutes or until browned. Sprinkle with paprika. Serve with celery sticks and prepared Hidden Valley Ranch Salad Dressing Mix.

HOGAN'S NUCLEAR CHICKEN WINGS

- 24 each Chicken Wings -- Separated
- 2 tablespoons Vegetable Oil
- 1/4 teaspoon Garlic Powder
- 3 tablespoons Habanero Sauce
- 3 tablespoons Tabasco Sauce
- Ground Red Pepper to taste
- 1 tablespoon White Vinegar
- 1/4 cup Brown Sugar
- 1 cup Bleu Cheese Salad Dressing
- Leaf Lettuce for platter

These chicken wings are quite easy to prepare. Adjust the amount of Tabasco sauce and Habanero sauce to your own tastes. I recommend though that you just cool them by dipping them in the bleu cheese salad dressing rather than decreasing the hot sauces.
Preheat oven to 375øF.
In a medium sized mixing bowl combine vegetable oil, garlic powder, Tabasco sauce, habanero sauce, vinegar and brown sugar.
Separate tips from wings.
Place tips and wings on cookie sheet(s).
Using a pastry brush, coat the wings with the sauce mixture.
Sprinkle ground red pepper over wings and tips.
Bake wings for 15 to 20 minutes or until browning has occurred.
Arrange wings on leaf lettuce and serve with your favorite beverage.
Dip wings in bleu cheese salad dressing for some cooling affect.
NOTE: These wings can also be cooked on the barbeque. Wings should be grilled for the same amount of time over medium high heat coals.

Home-Made Hot Wings

    2 1/2 pounds   Chicken Wings (12 to 15)
    6   tablespoons (3oz) Texas Pete Hot Sauce *
    4   tablespoons (2oz) Butter or Margarine

* For REAL spicy wing, use Tabasco Sauce Cut wings at all joints. Discard wing tips. Place the 24 to 30 pieces in absorbent paper towels to dry.
DEEP FRYER: 375ø 8-10 mins or until crispy.
OVEN: Spread wings in single layer on cookie sheet. Bake at 450ø for 25 mins.
Melt butter/margarine in sauce pan. Add hot sauce and stir well. Place cooked wings in covered bowl. Pour sauce over wings. Place lid on bowl and bowl. Place on plate covered with paper towel. Serve immediately.

HONEY MUSTARD WINGS

1	package	Campbell's Dry Onion with -- Chicken Broth Soup a Mix
1/3	cup	Honey
2	tablespoons	Spicy-brown mustard
18		Chicken wings

1. In large bowl, mix soup mix, honey and mustard. Set aside.
2. Cut wings at joints and discard tips. Add to soup mixture. Toss to coat.
3. Place chicken in baking pan. Bake at 400'F. 45 minutes or until chicken is done, turning once.

Hot 'n' Sassy Buffalo "Wings"

1 1/2	cups	Oats -- uncooked
2	teaspoons	Paprika
1	teaspoon	Garlic powder
1	teaspoon	Salt
3		Egg whites
3	tablespoons	Red pepper sauce
3		Chicken breasts -- cut in stri
		No stick cooking spray
1/4	cup	Yogurt -- plain low-fat
1/4	cup	Blue cheese dressing

Blend dry ingredients in blender or food processor about 1 minute; place in shallow dish. in another dish, beat egg whites and pepper sauce. Lightly coat chicken strips W/ oat mixture; shake off excess. Dip into egg mixture; then again with oat mixture. Place on rack of broiler pan. spray evenly with no-stick cooking spray to coat completely, about 20 seconds. Broil about 4 inches from heat for 3 minutes. Remove completely from oven. Turn chicken pieces over; spray with no-stick cooking spray to coat, about 20 seconds. Broil 2 to 3 minutes or until golden brown. Combine yogurt and dressing. Serve as dip with chicken and celery sticks

Hot 'n' Spicy Chicken Wings With Blue Cheese

```
                -----dip-----
  1/2  cup         sour cream
  1/2  cup         mayonnaise
  2    teaspoons   white wine vinegar
  1    tablespoon  chopped fresh parsley
  1    tablespoon  chopped green onions
  1/2  teaspoon    minced garlic
  1/2  teaspoon    tabasco pepper sauce
  3    tablespoons crumbled blue cheese
                salt & pepper to taste
                -----chicken wings-----
  12              chicken wings
                vegetable oil for frying
  4    tablespoons  melted butter or margarine
  1    teaspoon     catsup
  1    teaspoon     tabasco pepper sauce
                celery sticks
```

In a bowl, beat together all of the dip ingredients until blended. Set aside. Remove the tips from the wings and discard. Separate the first and second joints of the wings with a sharp knife. Pat the wings dry with paper towels. In a heavy saucepan, heat about 2 inches of oil to 350F on a deep-frying thermometer. Fry the wings. a few at a time, for about 6 minutes, until golden brown on all sides. Drain on paper towels. In a small bowl, mix the butter, catsup and Tabasco sauce. Toss the wings in the butter mixture to coat thoroughly. Serve hot, and pass the dip and celery sticks..

Hot And Spicy Chicken Wings

1	can	tomato sauce (8oz)
2	tablespoons	red pepper flakes
2	tablespoons	hot sauce
1	tablespoon	garlic powder
1	tablespoon	onion powder
2	tablespoons	jalapeno peppers -- chopped
1	pound	chicken wings

Combine tomato sauce, red pepper flakes, hot sauce, garlic powder, onion powder and Jalapeno peppers in a medium size bowl. Spray a baking sheet with no-stick cooking spray. Place chicken wings on baking dish. Brush sauce over wings. Bake at 350 for 20 mins. Turn over and brush with sauce and bake for another 10 mins. Serve with blue cheese dressing and celery if desired. Serves 4.

HOT CHICKEN WINGS

2 1/2 pounds	Chicken wings
	Oil for frying (optional)
6 ounces	Hot sauce or Tabasco
1/2 cup	Melted butter

Cut the chicken wings in two at the joints. In a large frying pan or skillet; heat to 360F enough oil (or shortening) to cover the chicken wings. Add the wings and fry until crisp, about 12-15 minutes.
To bake, preheat the oven to 450F. Spread the chicken wings out on a baking sheet in one layer and bake 45 minutes.
To make the sauce, combine the Hot Sauce or Tabasco and melted butter and blend thoroughly. As soon as the chicken wings are cooked, douse with the sauce, and serve immediately.
Serves 2-6 Nathalie Dupree's "New Southern Cooking" Nathalie says, "These little wings make a good meal for two or are a great appetizer. Up North, they are called Buffalo wings and are served with celery and blue-cheese dressing. The little wing tips should be trimmed off to make neater pieces. But I cook them along with the wings and save them for myself. I call them the "cook's treat." You may fry or bake the wings, depending on dietary considerations.

Hot Chicken Wings 1

3	pounds	Chicken wings
4	packages	Taco seasoning mix
		Flour
		Oil
		Celery stalks
		Blue cheese dressing

Mix together the flour and taco seasoning, get oil hot in pan. Flour chicken wings and fry until done. Serve with celery and blue cheese for dipping.

Hot Chicken Wings 2

```
 2 1/2  pounds      Chicken wings
                    Oil -- for frying (optional
  6     ounces      Hot sauce or tabasco
  1/2   cup         Melted butter
```

Cut the chicken wings in two at the joints. In a large frying pan o skillet; heat to 360F enough oil (or shortening) to cover the chicken wings. Add the wings and fry until crisp, about 12-15 minutes. To bake, preheat the oven to 450F. Spread the chicken wings out on a baking sheet in one layer and bake 45 minutes. To make the sauce, combine the Hot Sauce or Tabasco and melted butter and blend thoroughly. As soon as the chicken wings are cooked, douse with the sauce, and serve immediately. Serves 2-6

Hot Fajita Wings With Guacamole

1/4	cup	honey
2	tablespoons	lime juice
2	tablespoons	chili powder
2	tablespoons	soy sauce
2 1/2	pounds	chicken wings -- shoulder midsection only -- cut apart
1	carton	(6 oz) frozen -- avocado dip, thawed;
1	cup	homemade guacamole

In a large plastic bag, mix honey, lime juice, chili powder, and soy sauce. Add wings; seal bag and mix to coat. Chill, turning occasionally, at least 1 hour or up to a day. Lift out wings and place in a single layer on racks in 2 broiler pans, each about 10 by 15 inches. Bake in a 450 degree oven 15 minutes. Turn pieces over and continue baking until browned, 25 to 30 minutes. (If making ahead, let cool, wrap airtight, and chill up to 1 day; serve at room temperature or reheat in a single layer in pans in a 350 degree oven for about 10 minutes.) Put wings on a platter. Place avocado dip in a bowl set on platter with the wings. Makes 8 to 10 appetizer servings. Per serving: 170 calories (53% from fat), 10 g fat (2.4 g saturated), 363 mg sodium, 29 mg cholesterol.

HOT WINGS

48		Chicken wings
	-----SAUCE-----	
1/4	pound	Butter -- 1 cube
12	ounces	Crystal hot sauce
2	ounces	Louisiana hot sauce
4	ounces	Tapatio hot sauce
2	ounces	Red Devil pepper sauce
2	ounces	Tabassco

Disjoint wings and discard tips. Arrange in baking pan and bake in 375 degree oven for 1 hour, until done. Meanwhile combine butter, and sauces in sauce. Heat and stir until butter is melted. Keep warm.
Remove wings from oven and dip in individually in sauce mixture. Place in serving dish. Pour remainder of sauce over the top. Left over sauce can be refrigerated and used again.
Note: Choices of hot sauces may vary. Adjust amount to taste. Be sure to use the Crystal hot sauce and adjust the others. Above recipe is quite hot, but tasty!

Hot Wings 2

- 1/2 cup butter -- margarine melted
- 1/4 cup hot pepper sauce
- 3 tablespoons vinegar
- 24 chicken drumettes

Preheat oven to 350. In small bowl, whisk together butter, pepper sauce and vinegar. Dip drumettes in butter mixture; arrange in single layer in large baking pan. Bake until chicken is browned, 30 to 40 minutes. Sprinkle with paprika. Serve with salad dressing and celery sticks.

Jamaican Chicken Wings

72		Chicken drummettes
		MARINADE
2		Scotch Bonnet peppers -- or
4		Jalapenos -- seeded
3	bn	Green onions
1	cup	Red wine vinegar
1	cup	Olive oil
1/2	cup	Soy sauce
1/2	cup	Dark rum
1/4	cup	Brown sugar
1	tablespoon	Fresh thyme
1	teaspoon	Each ground cloves, nutmeg -- allspice and cinnamo

Blend all marinade ingredients in a blender. Marinate chicken wings overnight. Use gallon plastic bags. Cook wings in a 350~ oven for 30 to 40 minutes. Baste frequently.

Jamaican Hot Wings

1	pound	Butter
8	ounces	Jamaican Jerk Spice
1/2	ounce	Tabasco Sauce
8	ounces	Tomato Juice
8	ounces	Un bleached Flour
5	pounds	Chicken Wings; Or Drumettes -- Fresh Not Frozen
		Oil For Frying

Jamaican jerk spice may be found in specialty food stores. Melt the butter in a 2-quart sauce pot over low heat. Add the jerk spice, Tabasco sauce, and tomato juice. Blend well and set aside. Rinse the wings under cold running water and pat dry with paper towels. Dust the wing with the flour and deep fry in a heavy pot or skillet in about 2-inches of hot oil until done. Place the cooked wings in the sauce mixture and allow to marinate just a few minutes.
Drain off any excess liquid. Serve immediately. Makes 40 to 50 Wings

Jamaican Jerk Chicken Wings

-----FOR THE MARINADE-----
- 1 Onion -- chopped
- 2/3 cup Scallions -- chopped
- 2 Garlic cloves
- 1/2 teaspoon Thyme -- crumbled
- 1 1/2 teaspoons Salt
- 1 1/2 teaspoons Ground allspice
- 1/4 teaspoon Nutmeg -- grated
- 1/2 teaspoon Cinnamon
- 1/4 cup Jalapeno pepper -- minced
- 1 teaspoon Black pepper
- 6 drops Tabasco sauce
- 2 tablespoons Soy sauce
- 1/4 cup Vegetable oil

-----ADD TO MARINADE-----
- 18 Chicken wings -- trimmed

Marinade: In a food processor or blender, puree all ingredients except for the wings. In a large shallow dish arrange the wings in one layer and spoon the marinade over them, rubbing it in (use rubber gloves).

Let them marinate, covered & chilled, turning them once, at least 1 hour, or preferably, overnight.

Arrange the wings in one layer on an oiled rack set over a foil-lined roasting pan, spoon the marinade over them & bake in the upper third of a preheated 450F oven, 30-35 minutes, or until they are cooked through.

James' World's Hottest Wings!

2	pounds	Chicken Wings cut up Buffalo -- style
6		Whole sorano chili peppers
6		Whole red chili peppers
10		Whole jalapeno peppers
2	cups	White wine
1		Bottle Tabasco Sauce
1/2		Bottle Worcestershire sauce
10	tablespoons	Cayenne pepper
10	tablespoons	Durkee red-hot sauce
1	tablespoon	Salt
3	tablespoons	Pepper
1/2	cup	Vinegar
1		Fire Extinguisher -- (Optional!) attempt to eat with -- an ulcer.

In a blender, carefully puree the peppers, wine, vinegar and all spices. Caution, the fumes are deadly and wear rubber gloves or your fingers will burn! Put the puree into a bowl and marinate the wings in the bowl in the fridge for 5 days. After 5 days, carefully remove the wings and broil them until cooked. Usually approx 15 mins (+/- 5 mins). Take the marinade, put it on the stove, add 1/4 cup sugar and heat to a boil. reduce until thick. Pour over wings and re-broil for about 5 more minutes, serve with soda water for maximum heat effect but keep plenty of ice water handy.

Janice Okun's Buffalo Wings

24		Chicken wings (4 lbs.)
		Salt -- optional
1	dash	Fresh gr. pepper -taste
4	cups	Peanut oil
4	tablespoons	Butter
4	tablespoons	Louisiana Hot Sauce
1	tablespoon	White vinegar
2 1/2	cups	Blue cheese dressing-CC
		Celery sticks

Cut off and discard the small tip of each wing.
Cut the main wing bone and second wing bone at the joint. Sprinkle the wings with salt, if desired, and pepper to taste. Heat the oil in a deep-fat fryer or large casserole. When it is quite hot, add half of the wings and cook about 10 minutes, stirring occasionally, when the chicken wings are golden brown and crisp, remove them and drain well. Add the remaining wings and cook about 10 minutes or until golden brown and crisp. Drain well.
Melt the butter in a saucepan and add 2 to 5 Tbsp. of the hot sauce and vinegar. Put the chicken wings on a warm serving platter and pour the butter mixture over them. Serve with blue cheese dressing and celery sticks.

Japanese Chicken Wings

2	pounds	Chicken wings
1/2	cup	Soy sauce
1/2	cup	Sake
1/4	cup	Sugar
1/4	teaspoon	Crushed red pepper
1		Garlic clove -- crushed
1 1/2	teaspoons	Fresh ginger root -- grated (do not use powdered ginger)

Cut each chicken wing into 3 parts, separating at the joints. (Freeze wing tips for another use). In a 12 x 8 inch baking dish, mix remaining ingredients. Add chicken wings and turn to coat well. Let marinate for 1 hour, turning occasionally. (Can be prepared in advance. Cover and refrigerate for up to 24 hours).
Preheat oven to 375 degrees. Bake chicken in marinade uncovered for 1 1/2 hours, turning occasionally. Serve warm or

Jerk Chicken Wings

24		Whole chicken wings -- (about 4 pounds)
8		Scallions -- cut into 1" piece
4		Fresh jalapeno peppers -- seeded and coarsely
2	tablespoons	Distilled white vinegar
1	tablespoon	Ground allspice
4		Garlic cloves -- chopped
2	teaspoons	Dried thyme
1	teaspoon	Salt
1/2	teaspoon	Freshly ground pepper
1/4	teaspoon	Cayenne
1/4	cup	Vegetable oil
		Lime wedges

1. Rinse chicken with cold water and pat dry. Cut off and discard pointed tip of each wing and halve wings at the main joint. 2. In a food processor, combine scallions, jalapeno peppers, vinegar, allspice, garlic, thyme, salt, pepper, and cayenne. Process until well blended. With machine on, slowly pour in oil and puree until a thick paste forms. 3. In a large bowl, combine chicken wings and jerk paste. Toss until wings are well coated. Cover and refrigerate overnight 4. Preheat broiler. Arrange wings on broiler pan about 6 inches from heat and broil, turning once, until nicely browned outside and cooked through, about 20 minutes total. Serve warm or at room temperature with lime wedges and lots of napkins. The name of this recipe is no reflection on the cook; jerk is a fiery Jamaican marinade for chicken, pork, or beef.

MARINATED CHICKEN WINGS

1	cup	Dry sherry
1/2	cup	Soy sauce
1/4	teaspoon	Garlic powder
1	teaspoon	Ground ginger
48		Chicken wings

1. In a large bowl combine sherry, soy sauce, garlic powder and ginger; set aside.
2. Disjoint chicken wings into 3 parts each. Discard the tip end or save to use for soup stock at a later time.
3. Marinate chicken pieces in sherry mixture in the refrigerator at least three hours, but not longer than 24 hours.
4. Arrange 20 pieces at a time in a single layer on a heat-resistant, non-metallic serving platter.
5. Heat, uncovered, in Microwave Oven 12 to 14 minutes or until chicken is well cooked. Turn chicken pieces over after 5 minutes.
6. Repeat with remaining pieces as needed.

Tip: Uncooked chicken pieces can either be stored in refrigerator for 2 to 3 days or may be frozen for 3 months. Cooked pieces may be reheated.

Maurice's Spicy Chicken Wings

40		Chicken drumettes
3/4	cup	Soy sauce
2/3	cup	Honey
4	teaspoons	Vegetable oil
3	tablespoons	Dry mustard

Put drumettes into a plastic bag. Mix remaining ingredients together and pour into the bag. Close bag securely and shake until chicken is well coated.
Refrigerate for at least 2 hours. Preheat oven to 375 degrees. Line a baking sheet with aluminum foil and place rack on top of baking sheet. Remove chicken from bag and place on the rack. Bake for 30 minutes, until wings are crisp and golden.

Mexican Chicken Wings

-----INGREDIENTS-----
- 1/2 cup   Corn oil
- 1/4 cup   Chili powder
- 1 teaspoon   Oregano
- 1 teaspoon   Ground cumin
- 12 ounces   Tortilla corn chips
- 1 pound   Chicken wings -- disjointed tips discarded

1. Preheat oven to 350F. In a small bowl, whisk together the oil, chili powder, oregano, and cumin to blend well. 2. Pulverize the tortilla chips in a food processor. Pour into a shallow bowl.
3. Dip the chicken pieces in the seasoned oil; then dredge in the ground chips until coated. Set on a foil-lined baking sheet and bake for 45 minutes, until browned and crisp outside and tender inside. Serve hot.

Mexican Wings

10	ounces	Hot Sauce -
1/2	cup	Margarine -- melted
1/4	cup	Catsup -
1	teaspoon	Chili Powder -
1	teaspoon	Ground Cumin seed -
1/2	teaspoon	Garlic Powder -
5	pounds	Large chicken wings -- split or not, tips c

1. Combine hot sauce margarine, catsup & spices and heat, stirring frequently.
2. Fry wings at 365 until crispy, about 6-9 minutes depending on size and equipment used.(Check under ANCHOR BAR HOT WINGS for good handling procedure of Wings)
3. Drain well 4. Toss the wings in hot sauce mixture

Mr. Food's Santa Fe Wings

  2 1/2 pounds   chicken wings -- split/tips removed
    1/2 cup   hot pepper sauce
    1/4 cup   butter -- (1/2 stick)
    1/4 cup   chili sauce
  1   teaspoon   chili powder

Preheat the oven to 425 degrees (F). Place the chicken wings in a large, ungreased baking dish and bake for 30 minutes or until cooked and crisp, turning halfway through the cooking. In a large microwave-safe bowl, combine the remaining ingredients and microwave on high power for 1 minute or until the butter is melted. Stir well, then add the wings and toss until well coated. Serve immediately.

Napa Valley Chicken Wings with Wine Dressing

8		Chicken wings
1/4	cup	Cornstarch
2	teaspoons	Salt
1/2	teaspoon	White pepper
		Oil -- for frying
		-----WINE DRESSING-----
1	cup	Olive oil
1	cup	Tarragon wine vinegar
3/4	cup	Dry white wine
1		Garlic clove -- mashed
1/2	teaspoon	Dry mustard
1/2	teaspoon	Sugar
1/2	teaspoon	Dried basil -- crushed
1/2	teaspoon	Dried oregano -- crushed
1/2	teaspoon	Dried tarragon -- crushed
		Salt -- pepper
1	small	Tomato; peeled -- seeded & thinly sliced crosswise
1/2	medium	Green bell pepper -- thinly sliced crossw
1/2	small	Onion -- thinly sliced in rin

Disjoint chicken wings, discarding bony tips. Push flesh to oney end of bone on remaining parts. With sharp knife, remove smaller bone in wing portion containing 2 bones. Press fleshy ends of chicken pieces to flatten so they will stand upright. Dredge chicken in cornstarch mixed with 2 teaspoons salt and white pepper. Set aside to dry 30 minutes. Heat oil to depth of 1/2 inch in heavy skillet and fry chicken until golden brown and tender, about 7 minutes on each side. Drain on paper towels and freeze or refrigerate if not to be used at once. To make dressing, combine oil, vinegar, wine, garlic, mustard, sugar, basil, oregano and tarragon. Season to taste with salt and pepper. Blend well. Combine tomato slices, green pepper and onion slices with dressing and mix well. To serve, bring chicken wings to room temperature and arrange upright over tomatoes in shallow casserole.

Olive Garden Chicken Spiedies

		Marinade
1/4	c	Olive oil
1/4	c	Red wine vinegar
2	ts	Sugar
10		Garlic -- mince
1	t	Dijon mustard
1/2	ts	Salt
1/2	ts	Pepper
1/2	ts	Dried tarragon
1/2	ts	Dried oregano
1 1/2	lb	Chicken breasts -- bone, skin - cut 1x1" squares
		Appetizer sauce
1	c	Mayonnaise
2	ts	Dijon mustard
1	t	Garlic -- mince
2	ts	Dried tarragon
1/2	c	Pineapple juice
		Vegetables
3	lg	Red bell peppers -- 1/2x1" -- 72 strips
2	lg	Green bell peppers -- 1/2x1" -- 48 strips
1	lg	Yellow onion -- 1/2x1"; -- 96 strips
24		8" bamboo skewers -- soak in -- the fridge over-nigh

MARINADE-Add all ingredients except the chicken to a non-aluminum mixing bowl and mix thoroughly until the sugar and salt are completely dissolved. Pound the chicken breast between sheets of waxed peper until an even thickness of 3/16" overall. Cut the chicken breast meat into 1" squares and add to the marinade, covering completely. Allow to marinate for 2 hours, refrigerated. Remove from the marinade after 2 hours and drain.
SPIEDIES-Assemble in the following order: red bell pepper, onion, chicken (folded into "C" shape on the skewer), green bell pepper, onion, chicken, alternately, finishing with a red pepper strip after the 4th piece of chicken on each skewer. Spread the skewered items out on each skewer, so they will cook quickly. Place the Spiedies on a grill or a griddle and cook approximately 1 minute per side, turning 4 times. Adjust the timing according to your equipment's heat output. Serve immediately, 4 per quest, with dipping sauce, about 1/4 c per serving.
SAUCE-Mix all ingredients together just until blended. Chill 1 to 2 hours to blend flavors. Serve cold.

ONO CHICKEN WINGS

1	cup	Soy sauce
1	cup	Pineapple juice
1		Clove garlic -- minced fine
2	tablespoons	Onion -- minced
1	teaspoon	Ginger -- grated
1/4	cup	Brown sugar
7	ounces	Beer
1/4	cup	Vegetable oil
5	pounds	Chicken wings
		Sesame seeds -- toasted

Cut off and discard the small tip of each wing. Cut main wing at joint. Combine first 8 ingredients and stir until dissolved. Pour over chicken and marinate overnight. Be sure sauce overs all pieces. Drain and save marinade. In large skillet, heat a small amount of oil and brown chicken on all sides over medium.

When brown, add 1/2 cup marinade; cover; reduce heat and simmer 15-20 minutes. Stir and add more marinade if necessary. May be cooked a day in advance and reheated in oven before serving. Add marinade to moisten before heating. Serve hot in a chafing dish.

Sprinkle with toasted sesame seeds if desired.

Oriental Chicken Wings

24		Chicken wings -- sectioned
2		Cloves garlic -- minced
1	tablespoon	Ketchup
1/2	cup	Honey
1/2	cup	Soy sauce
1/2	cup	Dijon mustard
1	tablespoon	Veg oil

Marinade Arrange in pan & bake 1/2 hour - turn and bake until brown.

Original Buffalo Wings

Oil for frying or baking
2 pounds chicken wings -- dis-jointed tips
1/4 cup butter
1/4 cup hot pepper sauce
1 tablespoon vinegar
1/2 cup blue cheese dressing;chunky
6 stalks celery -- cut into 3" dipping sticks

IF DEEP FRYING, PLACE OIL IN A LARGE SKILLET AND HEAT TO 400 DEGREES. PLACE WINGS IN HOT OIL AND COOK 12 TO 14 MINUTES OR UNTIL GOLDEN BROWN. OR PREHEAT OVEN TO 450 AND PLACE 1/4 CUP OIL IN A 9 X 13 BAKING PAN. PLACE CHICKEN IN PAN AND BAKE FOR 30 TO 35 MINUTES OR UNTIL CRISPY. MEANWHILE, IN A MEDIUM SAUCEPAN, MELT BUTTER AND ADD HOT SAUCE AND VINEGAR. MIX WELL. SET ASIDE. WHEN WINGS ARE COOKED, REMOVE FROM SKILLET OR OVEN, PLACE WINGS IN A PLASTIC CONTAINER AND ADD SAUCE. COVER AND SHAKE VIGOROUSLY UNTIL WINGS ARE COATED WELL. REMOVE WINGS TO A SERVING TRAY AND GARNISH WITH BLUE CHEESE DRESSING AND CELERY STICKS. *COOK'S NOTE* FOR A HOTTER SAUCE, ADD 1/2 TEASPOON OF CAYENNE PEPPER TO THE BUTTER, HOT SAUCE AND VINEGAR.
FOR MILDER USE FAVORITE BARBECUE SAUCE INSTEAD OF HOT SAUCE.

Parmesan Chicken Wings

1	cup	Freshly grated parmesan cheese
1	tablespoon	Heaping -- finely chopped fresh Parsley
1	tablespoon	Fresh -- oregano or marjam Chopped
1	teaspoon	Salt
1/2	teaspoon	Fresh ground pepper
2	pounds	Chicken wings cut up
1/2	cup	Butter melted

Preheat oven to 375 deg. Mix cheese,parsley,oregano,salt and pepper together and place on a dry tray. Dip each piece of chicken into the butter,then roll in the cheese mixture,coating well. Place on a greased baking sheet. Bake for 45 minutes,turning when brown. Wings will freeze well. Thaw in refrigerator,and heat in a 375 deg. oven. Makes 4 main course or 8 appetizer servings...

Parmesan Chicken Wings Oreganata

1	cup	grated parmesan cheese (4oz)
2	tablespoons	chopped parsley
2	teaspoons	paprika
1	teaspoon	dried oregano
1/2	teaspoon	dried basil
1/4	teaspoon	salt
1/4	teaspoon	freshly ground pepper
1/2	cup	butter -- melted
1	pound	chicken wings -- disjointed tips removed

1. Preheat oven to 350F. In a paper bag, combine cheese, parsley, paprika, oregano, basil, salt, and pepper. Toss to mix. Pour melted butter in a shallow bowl.

2. Dip chicken pieces into butter, then place in a paper bag and shake to coat. Place chicken on foil-lined baking sheet and bake 45 minutes.

Serve hot.

Peanut Chicken Wings

50		Chicken wings
1/4	cup	Prepared mustard
2		12 oz bottles beer
3/4	teaspoon	Salt
1	cup	Molasses
2 1/2	tablespoons	Chili powder
3/4	cup	Peanut butter -- creamy style
1/4	cup	Chopped parsley for garnish
1/2	cup	Lemon juice
1 1/2		Lemons for garnish
1/2	cup	Worcestershire sauce

Preheat oven to 450. Get rid of the wing tips and cut each wing into two pieces. Combine remaining ingredients except parsely and lemon in a saucepan. Over low heat cook for about 15 minutes until reduced and thickened to the consistency of thick gravy. Place wings in a shallow baking pan and cover with sauce, making sure each is well coated. Bake for 15-20 minutes. Garnish with the green and yellow stuff.

Pop's Buffalo Wings

50	each	Chicken wing pieces
1/4	pound	Margarine
1/4	cup	Hot sauce
1	pinch	Cayenne pepper
1	pinch	Garlic salt
		Oil/fat for deep frying
		Black pepper
1	dash	Paprika
		Celery sticks
		Blue Cheese Dip

Deep fry the wing pieces(in small batches) in hot oil at 385 deg for 10 minutes, or follow package directions. Drain on paper towels; sprinkle with black pepper while draining. While chicken is frying, melt margarine in large skillet; mix in hot sauce, garlic salt, and cayenne. As Chicken is drained, toss into the sauce skillet and mix in. When all chicken is in the sauce, dash in paprika, mix again and allow to stand for a while. Reheat before serving. Serve with celery sticks and Blue Cheese Dip.

Puffed Chicken Wings

12		Chicken Wings
		-----MARINADE-----
1	teaspoon	Garlic -- minced
1	teaspoon	Gingerrroot -- minced
1/2	cup	Dry Sherry
2	tablespoons	Sesame oil
		-----BATTER-----
1/2	cup	Cornstarch
1/2	cup	Flour
1/4	teaspoon	Baking powder
1		Egg -- lightly beaten
1/2	cup	Milk

Add wings to marinade for at least one hour. Combine dry ingredients, stir in egg and milk. Pat wings dry.
Dip in batter. Drip off excess. Heat oil 350. Fry few wings at a time, 3-4 minutes.

Ranch Wings

  1 1/2 pounds   Chicken wings
    2/3 cup   Finely crushed round cracker
    1/2 teaspoon   Salt
  2   tablespoons Bottled Ranch Dressing
    1/2 teaspoon   Paprika

Cut off wing tips at joint. Cut each wing in half at joint. In a small bowl,toss chicken and dressing. On waxed paper,combine crushed crackers,paprika and salt;coat chicken with cracker mixture. In a 12 x 8" baking dish ,covered with a paper towel,on high microwave 7 to 9 minutes until chicken juices run clear when tested with a knife;rearrange halfway through cooking. If you desire,serve with additional Ranch dressing.

RAY'S ATOMIC WINGS

3 - 4 lbs of chicken wings -- cut up, washed throughly wing tips removed.
1   Lg bottle Durkee hot sauce
1   Cube butter
2   tablespoons   Smoke hickory flavor
1   tablespoon   Worcestershire sauce
1 1/4 teaspoons   Horseradish
1 1/4 teaspoons   Crushed garlic
 1/4 teaspoon   Salt
 1/4 teaspoon   Pepper -- to taste
3   cups   Oil

After cutting up chicken and washing, make sure chicken is dried off before deep frying. Also, season the parts with a little season salt before deep frying. Fry chicken parts for about 10 minutes per batch or golden brown.
After you've cooked all of them, dry off all oil from cooking. SAUCE: Mix the Durkee sauce with melted butter, salt & pepper, Worcestershire, smoke and crushed garlic in a saucepan until ingredients are mixed well; over low heat. Pull off stove and dip each chicken wing part in sauce and lay them in a casserole pan. Any left over sauce can be poured over wings. Bake in oven at 350 degrees for 45 to 60 minutes. Cover with foil when baking.

Rosemary Chicken Wings

- 2 tablespoons   Olive oil
- 2 tablespoons   Butter
- 2 tablespoons   Finely chopped shallots
- 2 teaspoons   Dried rosemary
- 1/2 cup   Lemonade
- 1 teaspoon   Black pepper
- 1 teaspoon   Salt
- 12   Chicken wings

Preheat oven to 425 degrees. In a small saucepan, heat oil and butter over medium heat. Add shallots and rosemary and cook 2 to 3 minutes. Add lemonade, pepper and salt. Simmer over low heat for 6 to 8 minutes or until slightly reduced and syrupy. Cool slightly.

Meanwhile, cut chicken wings into three pieces, discarding wing-tip joint. Place wings in shallow pan and coat well with sauce. Bake in oven until skin is golden brown, about 30 minutes. Serve with rice or as hors d'oeuvre. Makes 20 to 24 pieces.

San Antonio Style Chicken Wings

12		Chicken wings
1	cup	Pace picante sauce
1/3	cup	Catsup
1/4	cup	Honey
1/4	teaspoon	Cumin -- ground
2/3	cup	Sour cream -- dairy

Cut wings in half at joints; discard wing tips.
Combine 1/3 cup of the picante sauce, catsup, honey and cumin; pour over chicken. Place in refrigerator; marinate at least 1 hour, turning once.
Drain chicken, reserving marinade. Place on rack of foil-lined broiler pan.
Bake at 375F. for 30 minutes. Brush chicken with reserved marinade; turn and bake, brushing generously with marinade every 10 minutes, until tender, about 30 minutes.* Place 6 inches from heat in preheated broiler; broil 2 to 3 minutes or until sauce looks dry. Turn; broil 2 to 3 minutes or until sauce looks dry. Spoon sour cream into small clear glass bowl; top with remaining 2/3 cup picante sauce. Serve with chicken.
Makes 24 appetizers.*At this point, chicken may be refrigerated up to 24 hours. To serve, place 6 inches from heat in preheated broiler; broil 4 to 5 minutes.
Turn; broil 4 to 5 minutes or until heated through.

Saucy Sweet Sour Chicken Wings

12	Chicken wings -- tips removed
	-----MARINADE-----
1/2 cup	Water
1/4 cup	Oil
3/4 cup	Sugar
1/4 cup	Ketchup
1/4 cup	Vinegar
1 teaspoon	Garlic salt
1/2 teaspoon	Instant chicken bouillon

Cut each wing in half; place in large resealable bag; add all marinade ingredients; seal bag. Turn bag to coat wings. Refrigerate at least 4 hours, up to 24 hours, turning bag occasionally. Heat oven to 375~. Drain chicken, reserving marinade. Place chicken on broiler pan. Bake 45-60 minutes, brushing occasionally with marinade. Discard any remaining marinade.

Sesame Chicken Wings

36		Chicken drumettes (bottom
2	teaspoons	Ground coriander
		Part of chicken wing)
3	tablespoons	Soy sauce
20	milliliters	Garlic
3	tablespoons	Fresh lemon juice
1		Inch fresh ginger -- peeled
2	tablespoons	Sesame oil
1		Onion -- quartered
2	tablespoons	Sugar
1	teaspoon	Red pepper flakes
1/2	cup	Sesame seeds (approx)
2	teaspoons	Salt

Wash the chicken pieces and pat dry. Place in a bowl. Combine the remaining ingredients except the sesame seeds in a blender and puree. Pour the mixture over the chicken and stir to coat all the pieces well. Refrigerate for at least 2 hours.

Remove the chicken from the marinade and sprinkle with the sesame seeds. Place under the broiler for 5 to 6 minutes on each side. Serve hot.

Makes 6 to 8 servings as hors d'oeuvres.

Spicy Barbecue Wings

1/2	pound	chicken wings
		-----bar-b-q sauce-----
1/2	cup	ketchup
1/2	cup	water
2	teaspoons	dijon mustard
1	teaspoon	salt
2	teaspoons	Louisiana hot sauce
1/2	teaspoon	chili powder
2		garlic cloves - minced
1/4	cup	lemon juice
1	tablespoon	brown sugar
2	tablespoons	oil
2	tablespoons	worcestershire sauce
1/4	teaspoon	cumin
1	teaspoon	black pepper
		oil for deep frying

This BBQ sauce is mild. If you like hotter wings, add more Louisiana hot sauce. In a large heavy saucepan, mix together BBQ sauce ingredients. Bring to a boil, then reduce heat and simmer for 15 mins. In a frypan or wok, heat oil to 375 F (190 C). Deep fry a few wings at a time, until they are cooked through, about 10-15 mins. Drain fried wings on absorbent towel. when all the wings are cooked, place them in the simmering BBQ sauce. Stir to coat and serve.

SPICY CAJUN STYLE BUFFALO WINGS

3	pounds	Chicken Wings
1		Bottle Kraft Spicy BBQ
1 1/2	teaspoons	Red Cayenne Pepper
1/4	teaspoon	Salt
2	teaspoons	Black Pepper
1/2	teaspoon	Garlic flakes -- minced
1	teaspoon	Onion flakes -- minced
3	tablespoons	Worcestershire Sauce
2	tablespoons	Green Dragon or Jalapeno Sau
1	tablespoon	Tabasco Sauce
1	tablespoon	Cajun Spice***

Chicken wings or small chicken legs; more wings or legs can be added if needed. Kraft BBq or K.C. Style sauce. ***Cajun Spice or Capt. Link's Cajun seasoning.

In a Crockpot; add chicken BBq Sauce, and all spices.

Stir and heat on low for 4 hours. To serve, I suggest you prepare a Cajun Rice Recipe, and after the Buffalo Wings are cooked, prepare the Rice, pour the Rice into a container or casserole dish, spread out evenly.

Spicy Chicken Wings

- 1 cup chopped onion
- 2 tablespoons ketchup
- 2 tablespoons orange juice
- 1 tablespoon +1 t rc tub margarine
- 1 tablespoon Worcester sauce
- 2 teaspoons honey
- 3 drops red pepper sauce
- 1 1/2 pounds chicken wings
- 1/4 teaspoon black pepper
- 1 cup diced celery
- 1/2 cup plain lowfat yogurt
- 3/4 ounce crumbled blue cheese
- 1 tablespoon +1 tsp rc mayonnaise

To prepare sauce, in medium bowl, combine all ingredients except wings and black pepper. Micro on high 4 minutes, stirring once. With sharp knife, remove skin from wings. Place in an 11 x 7" baking pan in a single layer; sprinkle with black pepper. Spoon Pour half the sauce over the wings. Micro on High 6 minutes. Turn wings over;spoon remaining sauce over wings. Micro on high 6 min. or until juices run clear when skin is pricked with a fork. To prepare dip, combine all ingred. in small bowl.

Sweet And Sour Chicken Wings

24	whole	chicken wings
1/2	teaspoon	salt
1/2	teaspoon	freshly ground black pepper
1/4	teaspoon	garlic powder
1/2	cup	ketchup
1/2	cup	vinegar
1/2	cup	sugar
1/2	cup	water

Preheat oven to 350 F. Season wings with salt, pepper and garlic powder. Place in a shallow baking dish and bake for 15 minutes. in a small saucepan, combine ketchup, vinegar, sugar an

Sweet Sour Chicken Wings

3	pounds	Chicken wings
		Garlic Salt
		Corn Starch
2		Beaten eggs
3/4	cup	Sugar
1/2	cup	Chicken broth
4	tablespoons	Catsup
4	tablespoons	Soy sauce
1/4	cup	Vinegar

Cut wings in three pieces. Cook wing tips in water (to cover) to make broth. Sprinkle chicken wings with garlic salt. Let stand one hour. Roll in cornstarch, then in beaten egg. Fry until brown and crisp. Put in single layer in flat pan. Make sauce with rest of ingredients, including broth made from chicken wing tips, cook until sugar melts, then pour over chicken wings. Bake at 325F about one hour. Baste and leave uncovered during last 15 minutes.

Taco Chicken Wings

2 1/2	pounds	chicken wings
1	env	taco seasoning mix *
2	cups	dry bread crumbs
1	jar	(16oz) taco sauce **

* 1-1/4 oz Old El Paso ** Old El Paso Remove wing tips and discard. Cut wings at joint. Combine bread crumbs and taco seasoning mix; mix well. Preheat oven to 375. Dip each chicken piece in taco sauce then roll in bread crumbs; coat thoroughly. Place on lightly greased baking sheet. Bake for 30-35 mins.

Tea-Smoked Chicken Wings

3	pounds	Chicken wings -- (16 wings)
3		Cl Garlic
1	tablespoon	Ginger root -- grated
1	tablespoon	Honey
3/4	cup	Soy sauce
1/2	cup	Sherry
1	cup	Brown sugar
1	cup	Lapsang souchong tea -- (loose
		Sesame seeds -- for garnish

1. Using a knife, separate the mini drumstick end of the wing and slice through between the joints. Cut the wing tip off and discard. (any good butcher will dot his for you.) Wash the chicken thoroughly and pat dry.

2. Using the metal blade of your processor, finely chop the garlic. Add the grated ginger root, honey, soy sauce, and sherry, processing for 20 to 30 seconds to blend. Pour the marinade in a 9-by-13-inch baking pan, and add the chicken wings. With a spoon, drizzle the marinade over all the wings. Cover and refrigerate for at least 2 hours, rotating the chicken wings at least once.

3. To smoke the chicken, choose a heavy steel or cast iron roasting pan or skillet with a tight fitting lid. Line the bottom of the pan with heavy duty aluminum foil. Sprinkle the brown sugar and tea on top of the foil. Place a cake rack in the skillet, over the sugar and tea mixture, and arrange the chicken wings on the rack.
Cover the pan or skillet with a lid (or heavy aluminum foil if the lid does not fit snugly). Turn on your kitchen exhaust fan. Turn the burner on high, and leave chicken on high heat for 30 minutes (see Note). Do not remove the lid to check. Turn off the heat after 30 minutes, and keep the chicken covered another 20 minutes.
Smoked chicken will keep for several days if well-wrapped and refrigerated.

Serves 6 to 8 as an appetizer.

Note: As with any recipe requiring a dish to be cooked at high heat, use caution. Since this dish does produce smoke, it is imperative to use your kitchen exhaust fan, and to have a pan or skillet with a tight fitting lid.

NOTES: Smoking with tea is a traditional Chinese approach to preparing chicken. To the Western eye, the darkened skin resembles Cajun-style cuisine. These flavorful, bite-size chicken wings make a delicious appetizer when served plain, or with your favorite mustard, peanut or teriyaki sauce.

TERIYAKI WING DINGS

1/3	cup	Lemon juice
1/4	cup	Catsup
1/4	cup	Soy sauce
1/4	cup	Vegetable oil
2	tablespoons	Brown sugar
1/4	teaspoon	Garlic powder
1/4	teaspoon	Pepper
3	pounds	Chicken wings

Remove wing tips and cut at joints.

Combine all ingredients; mix well; add chicken. Cover and refrigerate at least 6 hours or overnight, turning occasionally. Preheat oven to 375F. Arrange chicken on rack in aluminum foil-lined shallow baking pan. Bake 40 to 45 minutes, basting occasionally with marinade.
Refrigerate leftovers. Enjoy!

THAI BBQ CHICKEN APPETIZERS

3	pounds	Chicken wing drummettes

-----MARINADE-----

1/4	cup	Coarsely chopped garlic
1	bn	Cilantro -- chop roots & lower s reserve leaves for garnish
1	teaspoon	Ground turmeric
1	teaspoon	Curry powder
1 1/2	teaspoons	Ground dried chilis -- - (cayenne or equiva
1	tablespoon	Sugar
1/4	teaspoon	Salt
3	tablespoons	Thai fish sauce -- - (filipino or vietnamese is ok -- too)

-----BASTING LIQUID-----

1/2	cup	Coconut milk (canned is ok)

-----DIPPING SAUCE-----

1/2	teaspoon	Dried chili flakes -- OR- cayenne
2		Garlic cloves -- - coarsely chopped
1	tablespoon	Brown sugar
1/4	teaspoon	Salt
1/2	cup	Chinese red rice vinegar
1		Green onion -- thinly sliced
1	tablespoon	Coarsely chopped cilantro -- - (leaves)

Preparation: Process all marinade ingredients in a blender until smooth. Marinate chicken, refrigerated, overnight. Grill over hot coals until done, brushing frequently with coconut milk. Serve garnished with cilantro sprigs, accompanied by steamed rice and bowls of dipping sauce.

DIPPING SAUCE: Pound first 4 ingredients to a paste with mortar and pestle, then dissolve in vinegar. Alternatively, put it all in a blender and blend until smooth. Float the green onions and cilantro on top.

WING-DING

		Chicken wings -- tips removed saved for stock!)
1 7/8	pints	Peanut oil
3/4	cup	Chili sauce -- commercial (hei
3	tablespoons	Lemon juice
3	tablespoons	Vinegar
1 1/2	tablespoons	Prepared yellow mustard
1 1/2	tablespoons	Worchestershire sauce (lea & -- perrins)
3/8	cup	Onion -- finely chopped
3/4	cup	Green bell pepper -- finely ch
3/4	teaspoon	Salt
3/4	teaspoon	Black pepper -- ground
3/8	teaspoon	Cayenne pepper

Make sauce by combining all ingredients except the wings & Peanut oil. Allow to marinade about 1 hour in the 'fridge. Split the chicken wings into sections. Coat in seasoned flour. Fry in peanut oil until done. Serve with the sauce on the side.

Zesty Orange Barbecued Chicken Wings

  12   Chicken wings -- tips removed
                -----MARINADE-----
  1/3 cup   Chili sauce
  1/4 cup   Orange marmalade
  1   tablespoon   Red wine vinegar
  1 1/2 teaspoons   Worcestershire sauce
  1/4 teaspoon   Garlic powder
  1/4 teaspoon   Prepared mustard

Cut each wing in half; place in large resealabe bag.
Add marinade ingredients; seal bag. Turn bag to coat wings. Refrigerate at least 4 hours or up to 24 hours, turning bag occasionally. Heat oven to 375~. Drain chicken, reserving marinade. Place chicken on broiler pan. Bake 45-60 minutes, brushing occasionally with marinade. Discard any remaining marinade.